This **PAWSITIVELY**
brilliant book belongs to:

_____

_____

PAW Patrol™: ANNUAL 2022
A CENTUM BOOK 978-1-913865-67-2
Published in Great Britain by Centum Books Ltd.
This edition published 2021.
1 3 5 7 9 10 8 6 4 2

books@centumbooksltd.co.uk

CENTUM BOOKS LIMITED. Reg. No. 07641486

A CIP catalogue record for this book is available from
the British Library.

Printed in China.

ANNUAL 2022

Centum

CONTENTS

Calling all PAW Patrol Fans! It's time For some PAWsome activity Fun!

This book is packed with pup-tastic puzzles, challenges and missions to complete, plus profiles of all your favourite pup pals and a fun story to share. So what are you waiting for? **Let's roll with the PAW Patrol!**

TRACK A TREAT!

There are 10 very special pup treats hidden on the pages throughout this book. **Colour in a treat each time you find one.**

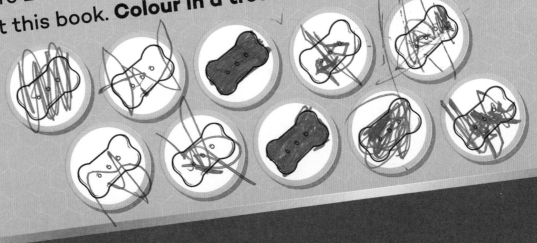

TO THE LOOKOUT!

There's an emergency in Adventure Bay! Ryder is calling the PAW Patrol to the Lookout, but his PupPad has gone wrong! It's mixed up all the pups' names! Can you help him unscramble them all?

A YKCOR

B LEBBUR

C MRSAAHLL

D HEASC

E YKSE

F MAZU

Write the correct name under each pup.

REPORTING FOR DUTY!

Ryder needs ALL the pups for the rescue mission, but someone is still missing. Who is it?

Tick off the pups as you spot them in the picture, then fill in the name of the missing pup.

The missing pup is:

_____

ANSWERS ON PAGE 74

9

PROFILE: MARSHALL

He's all fired up!

NAME: Marshall

BREED: Dalmatian

ROLE: Fire pup and Medic pup

UNIFORM COLOUR: Red

GADGETS:
Pup Pack with a double-spray fire hose

VEHICLE: Fire engine

SKILLS: Putting out fires, rescuing animals, medical help

CATCHPHRASE:

READY FOR A RUFF-RUFF RESCUE!

DID YOU KNOW?

Marshall's medical supplies include an X-ray screen to check pups and people for injuries!

MYSTERY MESSAGE

Ryder has sent a coded message to Marshall.
Circle every other letter to find out what it says.
The first letter has been circled to start you off.

F G I H R B E W C F O G M H E Y Q U U A I O C P K L

Write the message here:

_ _ _ _ _ _ ! / _ _ _ _ / _ _ _ _ _ !

HAT MATCH!

Each pup has a special uniform and hat to wear on rescue missions. Draw lines to match each pup with their hat.

Circle the pup with no hat and draw it for them here.

CHASE IS ON THE CASE!

Help Chase to reach the Lookout in super-quick time. Choose the path with the fewest cones blocking his way!

ANSWERS ON PAGE 74

13

PUPS-IN-TRAINING

Ryder is helping the pups practise for their next mission. Can you find the objects in the scene?
Colour a bone for each object you spot.

What's the name of the PAW Patrol headquarters?
Tick your answer:

The Pup Palace ☐   **The Lookout** ☐   **The Watchtower** ☐

Part 1

PUPPY BIRTHDAY TO YOU!

One windy afternoon in Adventure Bay, a box moved down the street toward Katie's Pet Parlour. But this box wasn't being blown by the wind. **It was creeping down the street on eight paws!**

Suddenly, a big gust blew the box away, revealing Skye and Rubble underneath. They quickly scampered into the shop.

Inside, Ryder, Katie and Rocky were getting ready for Chase's surprise birthday party. 'Who's making sure Chase doesn't surprise us while we set up?' Skye asked.

'Marshall,' Rocky said. 'He can keep a secret – can't he?'

Across town, Marshall and Chase were playing in the Pup Park. They swung on the swings and slid down the slide.

'Maybe we should go find Ryder and the pups,' Chase said.

CONTINUED ON **PAGE 28**

PROFILE: CHASE

His NOSE knows!

NAME: Chase

BREED: German Shepherd

ROLE: Police pup and Spy pup

UNIFORM COLOUR: Blue

GADGETS: Pup Pack with megaphone, searchlight and a net that can shoot out to catch things

VEHICLE: Police truck

SKILLS: Directing traffic, blocking dangers, solving mysteries

CATCHPHRASE:

CHASE IS ON THE CASE!

DID YOU KNOW?

Chase can sniff out anything – but he's allergic to cats and feathers!

SPOT THE DIFFERENCE

Chase is an expert at catching things with his net!
Can you spot 5 differences between these two
pictures of the police pup in action?

Colour in a star each time you find a difference.

ANSWERS ON **PAGE 74**

19

TRUCK TROUBLE!

Trace along the paths without touching the sides to help the pups reach their vehicles, so they can zoom to the rescue.

If you touch the sides, try again using a different coloured pen.

PUP TO PUP!

Draw lines to match the pup pairs. Which pup does not have a match?

Write the pup's name here:

BRILLIANT BADGES

Each pup has a special badge, which shows what they do best. Create your very own badge by tracing over the shape below, then drawing a picture in the middle.

Draw something that shows what you like to do best!

SHADOW SHAPES

Draw lines to match the pups to their shadows!

Which pup do you think this shadow belongs to?

_____

ANSWERS ON **PAGE 75**

FRIENDS FOREVER!

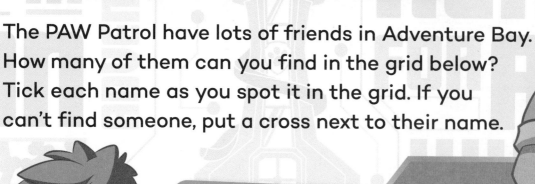

The PAW Patrol have lots of friends in Adventure Bay.
How many of them can you find in the grid below?
Tick each name as you spot it in the grid. If you
can't find someone, put a cross next to their name.

F	T	I	C	A	L	I	O	S	C
A	H	V	H	S	J	A	K	E	A
R	M	R	P	O	R	T	E	R	P
M	J	G	C	R	S	A	Y	B	N
E	W	A	L	L	Y	G	I	E	T
R	G	V	I	K	O	P	A	T	U
Y	A	H	C	E	K	G	T	R
U	D	W	H	P	R	U	I	B
M	N	H	V	D	Q	X	N	O
I	W	O	N	A	T

- [ ] **KATIE**
- [ ] **ALEX**
- [ ] **JAKE**
- [ ] **MR PORTER**
- [ ] **FARMER YUMI**
- [ ] **BETTINA**
- [ ] **CALI**
- [ ] **WALLY**
- [ ] **CAP'N TURBOT**
- [ ] **CHICKALETTA**
- [ ] **MAYOR GOODWAY**

CLUE!
There are two names missing from the grid!

ANSWERS ON **PAGE 75**

TIME FOR A TREAT!

Draw lines to match each pup with their food bowl.
Then test out your spotting skills by answering the questions.

1 **Which pup has the most treats?** _____

2 **Which pup has a green bowl?** _____

3 **Which pup's bowl contains just yellow treats?** _____

4 **Who has the most red treats?** _____

PROFILE: RUBBLE

Let's dig it!

NAME: Rubble

BREED: Bulldog

ROLE: Construction pup

UNIFORM COLOUR: Yellow

GADGETS: Pup Pack with a bucket arm scoop

VEHICLE: Digger with a bucket shovel and drill

SKILLS: Building, digging, lifting and transporting heavy things

CATCHPHRASE:

HERE COMES RUBBLE ON THE DOUBLE!

DID YOU KNOW?

Rubble loves to get covered in mud and then visit Katie's Pet Parlour for a warm bubble bath!

DOTTY ABOUT DIGGING

Rubble just loves to dig! **Join the dots** to complete his bucket scoop arm, so he can get to work right away.

Now colour in your picture of the construction pup.

27

PUPPY BIRTHDAY TO YOU!

Part 2
Read Part 1
on **pages 16–17**

'No!' Marshall protested. 'We can't! Because it's, um, so nice out.'

Just then, the wind picked up again and blew them right across the park!

Back at the Pet Parlour, the lights suddenly went dark, and Katie's mixer stopped.

'All the lights on the street are out!' Rocky yelped.

Ryder thought he knew what was wrong.

'PAW Patrol, to the Lookout!'

28

The team raced to the Lookout. But without electricity, the doors wouldn't open. Luckily, Rocky had a screwdriver, which did the trick.

Once they were inside, Ryder used his telescope to check Adventure Bay's windmills.

'Just as I thought,' he said. 'The wind broke a propeller. Since the windmill can't turn, it can't make electricity. We need to fix it!'

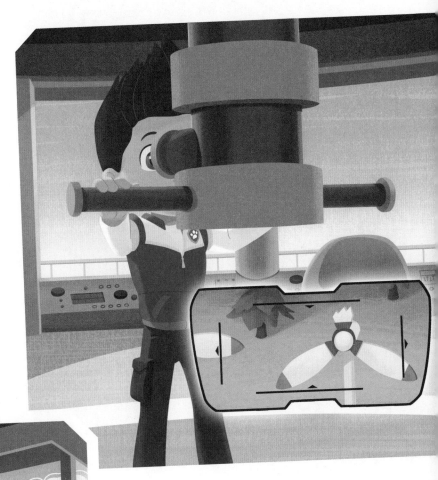

Ryder looked at Rocky. 'We'll need something from your truck to fix the broken blade.'

'Green means go!' Rocky said, preparing for action.

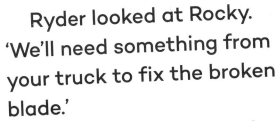

CONTINUED ON **PAGE 48**

29

PUP PUZZLE

How well do you know the PAW Patrol pups? Draw circles around the wrong statements as quickly as you can. **Get ready, set, go!**

Marshall is a police pup.

For an ocean rescue, call on **Zuma**.

Rubble is a German Shepherd dog.

Chase wears a green uniform.

Everest is amazing at snowboarding.

ANSWERS ON **PAGE 75**

30

I SPY!

The pups are enjoying a day at the beach.

Can you find ...

3 seagulls
☐

2 boats
☐

4 bottles
☐

An ice cream
☐

A surfboard
☐

A racket and ball
☐

Tick the boxes as you find each thing.

31

ANSWERS ON **PAGE 75**

TO THE RESCUE

Pick the items you would choose for these pup-tastic challenges.

1 Ryder needs to get a message to the pups quickly. **What would work best?**

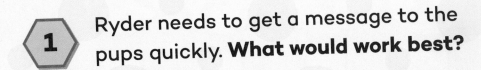

A   B   C

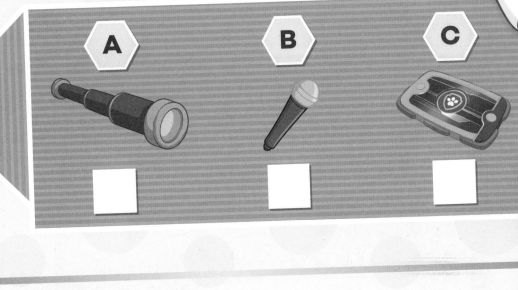

2 Rocky needs to fix some dangerously loose nails in a go-kart. **What does he need from his pack?**

A   B   C

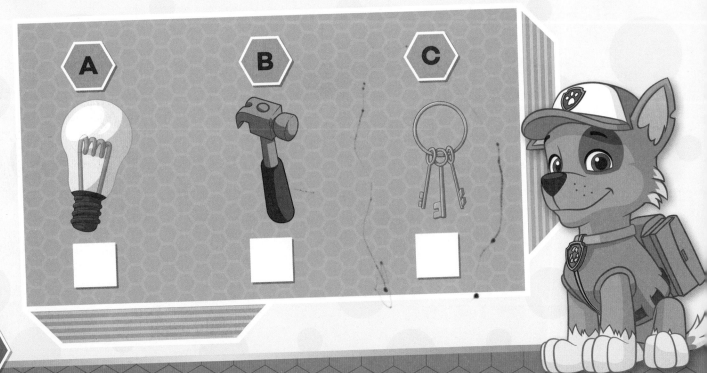

3 Help! The pups have an emergency in deep snow.
Which vehicle can get there?

A ☐

B ☐

C ☐

4 Cali is stuck in a tall tree and only Marshall can help.
What item should he use?

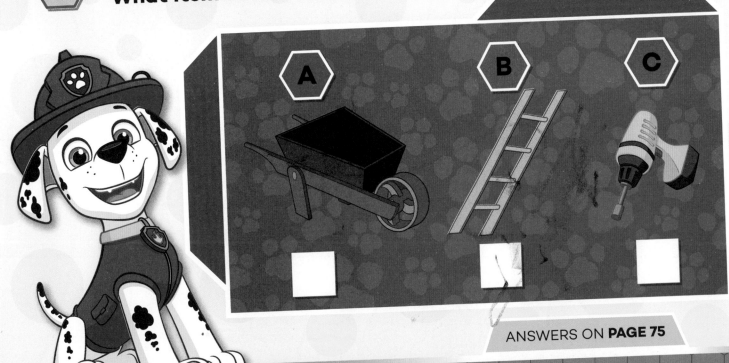

A

B

C

☐ ☐ ☐

ANSWERS ON **PAGE 75**

ON A COLOUR ROLL

Colour this picture of Ryder and Rubble – using a dice! You will also need yellow, blue, green, red and brown pens. Choose the area you will colour then roll a dice to find out what pen colour to use.
See what wild picture you end up with!

COLOURS

YELLOW

RED

BLUE

BROWN

GREEN

LEAVE WHITE

SPOT THE ODD PUP OUT

The pups practise their skills and train every day to be the very best they can. Practise your skills by finding the odd pup out in each row.

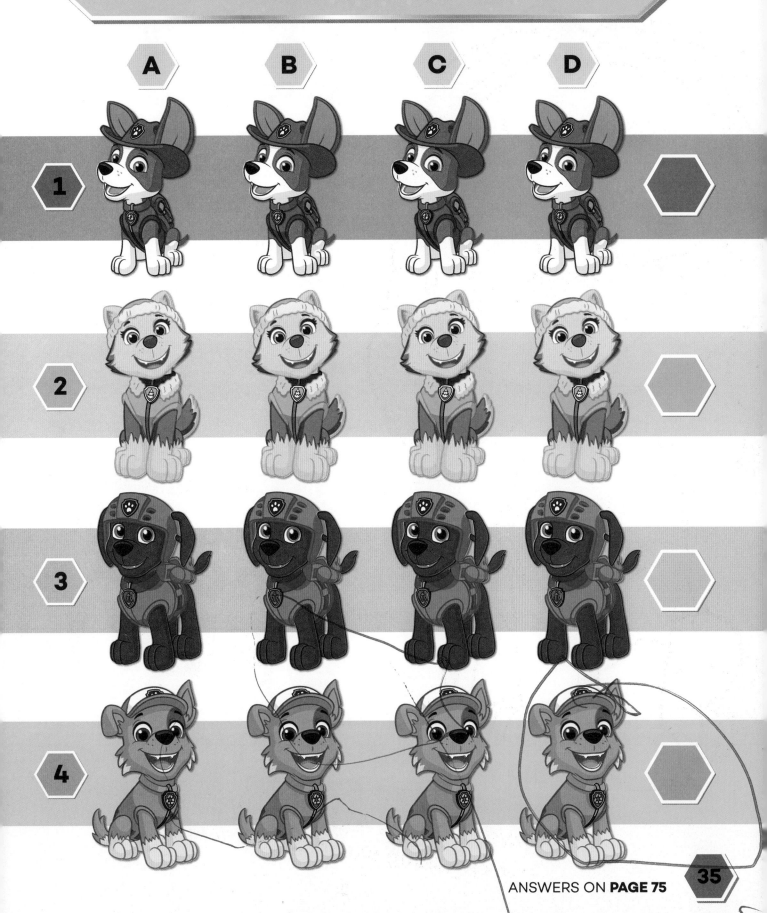

PROFILE: SKYE

Pups away!

NAME: Skye

BREED: Cockapoo

ROLE: Pilot pup

UNIFORM COLOUR: Pink

GADGETS: Pup Pack with wings that allow her to take flight

VEHICLE: Helicopter

SKILLS: Flying, flips and spins!

CATCHPHRASE:

THIS PUP'S GOTTA FLY!

DID YOU KNOW?

Skye is really brave and very little frightens her, but one thing she is afraid of is eagles.

SKY HIGH

Alex's kite has blown away on the breeze. Help Skye find her way through the clouds to rescue it.

How many birds does Skye meet on her way?

ANSWERS ON **PAGE 75**

ON THE FARM

The pups are helping Farmer Yumi as she prepares Mr Porter's weekly delivery. Can you answer the questions about the scene?

1 How many **LAMBS** are in the picture?

2 Which **DIGGER PUP** is missing?

3 How many **CARROTS** can you count?

4 There is a pile of another type of **VEGETABLE** – what is it?

5 What kind of **BUG** can you spot in the picture?

Can you spot these pictures in the scene? **Tick them when you find them.**

ANSWERS ON **PAGE 76**

PICK A PUP

Help Ryder pick a pup for each of these missions. Draw lines to match the pups to the missions.

1 Stunt pilot, Ace Soarensen, is in trouble in the sky.

2 There's a mountain of rubbish to sort and recycle.

3 Precious's boat is out of control on the water.

4 Jake has slipped and fallen on an icy mountain.

40

ANSWERS ON PAGE 76

RUBBLE ON THE DOUBLE

Complete this picture of Rubble by drawing the missing half of his face in the grid. Then finish colouring him in so the two sides match.

SEEK AND FIND

The pups are all searching for different things. Can you help them? Tick each item on the list when you have found it.

 Chase is searching for his Pup House. ☐

 Skye wants a pup treat. ☐

 Rubble wants some pizza. ☐

 Rocky is looking for a bin. ☐

 Zuma is looking for Wally. ☐

 Everest needs her snowboard. ☐

 Marshall needs his bowl. ☐

 Tracker is sniffing out a snake. ☐

ANSWERS ON **PAGE 76**

ALL PAWS ON DECK!

Draw lines to match the missing pieces
to the picture to complete it.

ANSWERS ON PAGE 76

PROFILE: ZUMA

Let's dive in!

NAME: Zuma

BREED: Labrador

ROLE: Water-rescue pup

UNIFORM COLOUR: Orange

GADGETS: Pup Pack with air tanks and propellers for diving and swimming underwater

VEHICLE: Hovercraft that can travel on land or water

SKILLS: Rescuing sea animals, underwater missions, water sports

CATCHPHRASE:

READY, SET, GET WET!

DID YOU KNOW?

Zuma's hovercraft can transform into a submarine for deep underwater adventures!

44

FISHY FRIENDS

Follow the instructions below to colour in Zuma's fishy friends and make a PAWsome underwater scene.

Colour **4** fish red.
Colour **3** fish yellow.
Colour **2** fish blue.
Colour **2** fish orange.
Colour **1** fish pink.

How many fish are there altogether?

_____

ADVENTURE BAY HANGOUT

Where would you most love to visit in Adventure Bay? **Try this game to find out.**

1 **Choose a toy.**
a. Yoyo
c. Skateboard
b. Teddy bear
d. Kite

2 **Pick an animal.**
a. Horse
c. Rabbit
b. Penguin
d. Seal

3 **Circle your favourite season.**
a. Spring
c. Autumn
b. Winter
d. Summer

4 Pick your favourite pup.
a. Marshall **b.** Everest
c. Rubble **d.** Zuma

5 Choose a colour.
a. Green **b.** Purple
c. Pink **d.** Yellow

Now count up your answers to find your hangout!

Mostly As

Farmer Yumi's Farm

Mostly Bs

Jake's Mountain

Mostly Cs

Katie's Pet Parlour

Mostly Ds

Adventure Bay Beach

PUPPY BIRTHDAY TO YOU!

'We'll need Marshall's ladder to climb up and fix the windmill,' said Ryder.

Marshall nodded. 'I'm fired up!'

'Chase, the traffic lights won't work without electricity,' Ryder continued. 'I need you to use your siren and megaphone to direct traffic.'

'These paws uphold the laws,' Chase declared.

Meanwhile, Skye, Zuma and Rubble raced back to the Pet Parlour to continue setting up for Chase's surprise party. It was very dark, but Katie had a torch.

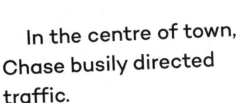

In the centre of town, Chase busily directed traffic.

'You're our hero,' Mayor Goodway said as she crossed the street safely.

'I'm just doing my PAW Patrol duty,' Chase said.

Up in the hills, Ryder, Marshall and Rocky went to work on the broken windmill. Ryder climbed Marshall's ladder and removed the old blade while Rocky looked for a replacement piece.

'No, not a tyre... not a garden chair,' Rocky said, pulling stuff out of his truck. At last he found what he wanted. 'Here it is – my old surfboard!'

CONTINUED ON **PAGE 56**

SWEET DREAMS

Marshall is snuggling down to go to sleep. Draw a picture of what he wants to dream about. Maybe it will be pup treats, or perhaps he will dream about a friend. It's up to you!

YOU MUST BE JOKING!

The PAW Patrol love to make their friends laugh.
Try out these **PAWsitively** hilarious jokes on your pals.

Q. What kind of dog is always on time?
A. A watch dog!

Q. What do you call a funny mountain?
A. Hill-arious!

Q. Where does a jungle pup get flowers from?
A. The rain-florest!

Q. What do you get when you cross a pup with a calculator?
A. A friend you can count on!

Q. What do you call young dogs that play in the snow?
A. Slush puppies!

PROFILE: ROCKY

Rocky to the rescue!

NAME: Rocky

BREED: Mixed breed

ROLE: Recycling pup

UNIFORM COLOUR: Green

GADGETS: Pup Pack with a mechanical claw and lots of handy tools

VEHICLE: Recycling truck

SKILLS: Creativity and ideas, fixing things, solving problems

CATCHPHRASE:

DON'T LOSE IT – REUSE IT!

DID YOU KNOW?

Rocky doesn't like getting wet at all, which means bath time isn't much fun!

TIDY UP TIME!

Rocky needs to sort out the rubbish for recycling. Can you help him by drawing lines to match up the items that are the same?

1 2 5 6 3 4 8 9 10 7 11 12 13 14

ANSWERS ON PAGE 76

SEASON ADVENTURES

Follow the pups through spring, summer, autumn and winter for fun and games galore.

SPRING

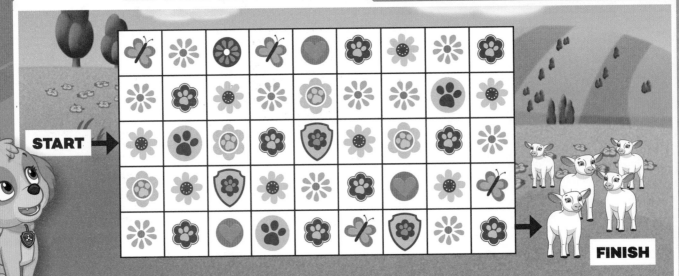

Skye is going to visit the farm to meet the new lambs.
Follow the flowers in the correct order to help her get there.

SUMMER

Marshall and Rubble are building a pup-tastic sandcastle. **How many new words can you make from the letters in SANDCASTLE?**

SANDCASTLE

cat

last

AUTUMN

It's harvest time and the pups are helping Farmer Yumi gather the pumpkins. **How many are there?**

WINTER

Chase and Skye are building a snowman on the slopes.
Can you spot five differences between the two pictures?

PUPPY BIRTHDAY TO YOU!

Part 4
Read Part 3
on pages 48-49

'This surfboard will catch a breeze and help turn it into electricity,' Rocky said as he bolted the board into place. The wind picked up and the windmill started to turn. Lights came on all over Adventure Bay!

The traffic lights started working again.

'Ryder and the PAW Patrol did it!' Chase announced through his megaphone. 'My work here is done!'

The lights in the Pet Parlour glowed brightly.

'Hooray!' cheered Skye, but then she frowned. 'Aw! There's no time to make a cake.'

Katie thought for a moment. 'I have an idea!'

As Chase drove back to the Lookout, he got a call from Ryder. 'We need you at Katie's – in a hurry!' When Chase got there, everything was dark and quiet.

Chase stepped inside. The lights went on.

'SURPRISE!' everyone yelled.

Chase was amazed. 'Wow! You guys turned the lights back on AND made a party for me?'

'We didn't have time to bake you a real cake,' Katie said, 'so we hope you like your pup-treat cookie cake.'

'Whenever it's your birthday, just yelp for help!' Ryder said with a laugh.

The End

RACE TO THE RESCUE

Get ready for a ruff-ruff rescue mission in Adventure Bay!

The railway track is blocked by a rockfall and the train can't get through! **Who will be the first to round up all the pups and get to the emergency first?**

13

12

11
MARSHALL is all fired up. **TAKE A SHORTCUT TO SQUARE 16!**

10

9

8

You will need:

- 2-4 players
- A coin counter for each player
- A dice

START HERE

1

2

CHASE is in his police uniform, ready to go! **MOVE FORWARD 5 SPACES**

3

4

5

RUBBLE has a road block to complete. **MOVE BACK 1 SPACE**

6

7
Wheeee! **EVEREST** is busy snowboarding. **MISS A TURN**

What to do:

- Place your coins on the **START** square.
- Take turns to roll the dice. Whoever is first to roll a 6 begins.
- Roll the dice and move that number of spaces on the board.
- If you land on an Action square, follow the instructions.
- The first to land on the **FINISH** square is the winner!

14

15

16

17

18

19

20

21

Uh-oh! **ZUMA** has an emergency at sea. **MOVE BACK 3 SPACES**

22

23

SKYE'S helicopter has got you in a spin! **CHOOSE SOMEONE TO SWAP PLACES WITH YOU**

24

25

ROCKY'S tools are ready for action. **MOVE FORWARD 1 SPACE**

26

27

28

FINISH

PROFILE: EVEREST

Born to slide!

NAME: Everest

BREED: Husky

ROLE: Mountain-rescue pup

UNIFORM COLOUR: Turquoise and yellow

GADGETS: Pup Pack with a grappling hook and foldable, rocket-powered snowboard

VEHICLE: Snowcat with a claw to grab large objects, and transport a sledge

SKILLS: Snowy rescues, climbing icy slopes, super-fast snowboarding

CATCHPHRASE:

ICE OR SNOW, I'M READY TO GO!

DID YOU KNOW?

Everest likes **belly-bogganing**, where she slides down the slopes on her belly!

DOT TO DOT

Everest is on her way to play with the penguins. **Join the dots** to complete her snowcat, then draw three penguins and colour in your picture.

HOME, SWEET HOME!

Draw lines to match each pup to their Pup House.
Now colour them in using the dots to help you.

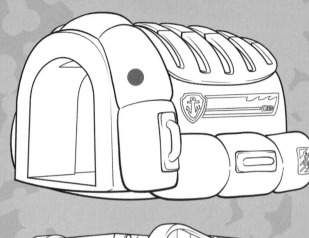

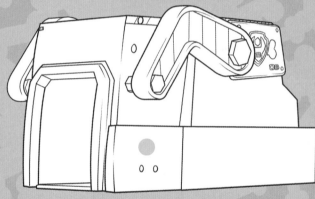

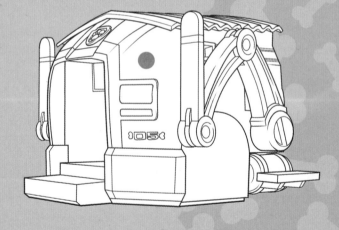

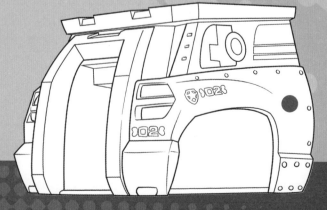

ANSWERS ON **PAGE 77**

IT'S PLAYTIME!

When they are not busy on rescue missions, the pups love to play together. **Try this PAWsome game** with one of your friends!

TIP: Use a pencil so you can rub it out and play again.

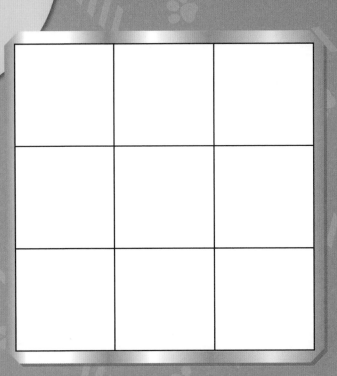

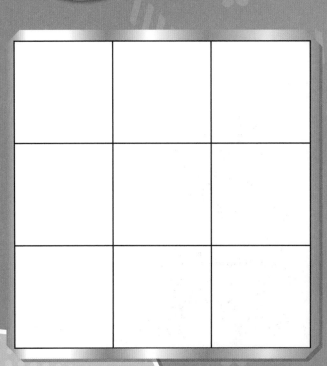

How to play:

1. Decide who will be the paw print and who will be the bone.
2. Take turns to draw your shape in the grid.
3. The first person to get three in a row wins the game!

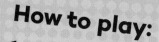

RUFF-RUFF COUNTING!

Help the pups to complete the tasks by drawing the correct number of things in each box.

Chase puts out 7 road cones.

Rocky places 4 plastic bottles in the bin.

Rubble finds a hammer and **10** nails.

Everest makes **6** snowballs.

UP CLOSE

Look carefully at these close ups. **Can you work out who they are?** Write the names underneath the pictures.

66

WORD PLAY

How many new words can you make using the letters in this phrase?

PAW PATROL, READY FOR ACTION!

Here are some words to get you started:

Red

Day

Pot

PROFILE: TRACKER

Buenos dias, PAW Patrol!

NAME: Tracker

BREED: Chihuahua

ROLE: Jungle-rescue pup

UNIFORM COLOUR: Green

GADGETS: Pup Pack with a compass, torch and grappling cables

VEHICLE: Jeep with a special radar tracking system

SKILLS: Jungle rescues, super-hearing (thanks to his big ears!)

CATCHPHRASE:
I'M ALL EARS!

DID YOU KNOW?

Tracker can speak two languages – **English and Spanish.**

TRACKER TIME

Tracker is on the trail of someone special. **Can you help the jungle pup sniff his way through the maze to find him?** Then answer the questions.

How many skunks did Tracker meet on the way?

Who did Tracker find?

What other creature is hiding in the jungle?

69

PAMPERED POOCH

Rubble is visiting Katie's Pet Parlour for some pampering!
Can you spot eight differences between these two pictures?
Colour in a paw print for every difference you spot.

ANSWERS ON **PAGE 77**

BEST PUP EVER!

Who's your favourite member of the PAW Patrol? **Draw a present for the lucky pup here** to say thank you for being such a pup-tastic hero. Don't forget to write their name on the label!

How about something yummy to eat, a new toy or an exciting storybook?

Dear.............................

Thank you for being so **PAWSOME!**

PUP PARTNER

The pups are all best friends, but which PAWsome pooch is your perfect match? **Try this quiz to find out!**

Your pup match is
RUBBLE

Your pup match is
SKYE

Your pup match is
ROCKY

Can you skateboard?

YES

Are you good at building things?

NO

YES — NO

YES

Would you like to ride in a helicopter?

Do you like playing video games?

NO — NO

YES

Are you great at fixing things?

Are you always thinking of new ideas?

YES — YES

START HERE

Would you be a good detective?

NO

YES

Is blue the best colour?

NO

YES

YES

Your pup match is
CHASE

Would you like to be a firefighter?

NO

YES

YES

Can you be a little clumsy?

YES

NO

NO

Your pup match is
MARSHALL

Are you the tallest in your group of friends?

NO

NO

Can you dive into water?

YES

Your pup match is
ZUMA

73

ANSWERS

P19

P8
A = ROCKY, B = RUBBLE,
C = MARSHALL,
D = CHASE, E = SKYE,
F = ZUMA

P9
The missing pup is Marshall.

P11
FIRE! COME QUICK!

P12

P13 Path B.

P21 Rocky doesn't have a match.

PAGES 14-15

PUPS-IN-TRAINING

Ryder is helping the pups practise for their next
mission. Can you find the objects in the scene?
Colour a bone for each object you spot.

What's the name of the PAW Patrol headquarters?
Tick your answer:

The Pup Palace ☐   The Lookout ✓   The Watchtower ☐

14

15   ANSWERS ON **PAGE 74**

P23

The shadow belongs to Skye.

P24

P25

1. Rubble, **2.** Rocky, **3.** Skye,
4. Marshall

P30

Marshall is a police pup.

For an ocean rescue, call on Zuma.

Rubble is a German Shepherd dog.

Chase wears a green uniform.

Everest is amazing at snowboarding.

PAGES 32-33 **1.** C, **2.** B, **3.** A, **4.** B

P35 **1.** B, **2.** C, **3.** A, **4.** D

P37 Skye meets 4 birds on her way.

P31

ANSWERS

PAGES 38-39

1. 3 lambs, **2.** Rubble,
3. 10 carrots, **4.** Pumpkins,
5. Ladybird.

P40

P42

P43

1. C, **2.** E, **3.** D, **4.** B, **5.** A.

P45

There are 12 fish in total.

P53

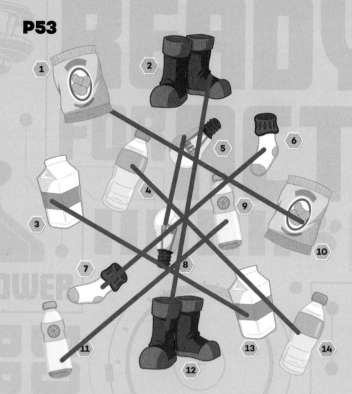

PAGES 54-55

Spring

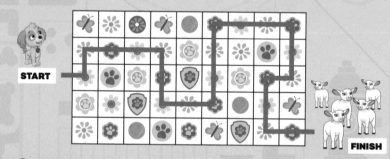

Autumn

17 pumpkins.

Winter

P62

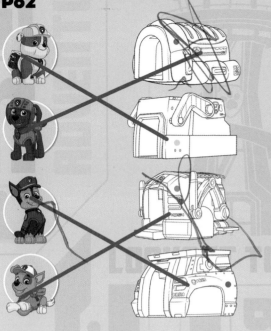

P70

P66

1. Skye, 2. Zuma, 3. Rocky,
4. Ryder, 5. Tracker

P69

Tracker met 3 skunks.
Tracker found Carlos
A snake is hiding in the jungle.

You will find the 10 pup treats hidden on pages 8, 13, 18, 24, 31, 40, 45, 59, 65, 71